Poetry, they're pretty sure you're not worth knowing,
fit for nothing, broken; that any mystery in language
perfected by its music's just a mockery, a joke;
outmoded as the nose flute; desperate as spite;
a series of temples raised to pretexts or a pimped-
out souped-up pussy-magnet; is anyway soaked
as a bandage and see-through; a piece of plastic
crap or encrypted chat, some intimate nightmare,
and they want you put to a phone-in vote . . . I don't.
One time I found you mooching round the back
of the loading dock at the meat factory, smoking
a rollie and eyeing the maggots writhing below
like disco rice, and recognized you from the fist
as work done by the soul's hands, sympathetic
magic that if profitless could still outstrip each
calculated want: and at the Moment of Death as
Described by the Upanishads, or in the lift of
pressure as you shift to third and open it up on
the last bend west out the Orritor Road, what
you offer is a juncture of the two kinds of real,
the act caught in the act, as the fingertips pressed
hard against their mirrored selves establish an
ambiguous exactitude – and if it so happens that
you are the flawed compensation for our having
just the one go, it does for me, or very nearly.

NICK LAIRD

Go Giants

W. W. Norton & Company
New York • London

For information about permission to reproduce selections from this book,
write to Permissions, W. W. Norton & Company, Inc.,
500 Fifth Avenue, New York, NY 10110

For information about special discounts for bulk purchases, please contact
W. W. Norton Special Sales at specialsales@wwnorton.com or 800-233-4830

Manufacturing by Courier Westford
Production manager: Louise Mattarelliano

Library of Congress Cataloging-in-Publication Data

Laird, Nick, 1975–
[Poems. Selections]
Go Giants / Nick Laird. — First American Edition.
pages cm
Poems.
ISBN 978-0-393-34744-9 (paperback)
I. Title.
PR6112.A35A6 2013b
821'.92—dc23

2013019964

W. W. Norton & Company, Inc.
500 Fifth Avenue, New York, N.Y. 10110
www.wwnorton.com

W. W. Norton & Company Ltd.
Castle House, 75/76 Wells Street, London W1T 3QT

1 2 3 4 5 6 7 8 9 0

If I were to describe reality as I found it, I would have to include my arm.

Acknowledgements

The book is dedicated to Carol Laird.

Thanks to the editors of the following publications where these poems or versions of them first appeared: *Dark Matter, Edinburgh Review, Guardian, Hear Here!, Literary Imagination, London Review of Books, Magma, Manchester Review, New York Review of Books, New Yorker, Ploughshares, Poetry Ireland, Poetry London* and *The Word Exchange: Anglo-Saxon Poems in Translation*.

Thanks to Matthew Hollis, Paul Keegan and Don Paterson. And thanks to Julian Barnes for the loan of two lines. And thanks unlimited to Z.

In the frontispiece poem, a 'series of temples raised to pretexts' is one of E. M. Cioran's descriptions of history. 'Envy' borrows from Bertrand Russell's *The Conquest of Happiness*, and the book's epigraph is a quotation from Russell's *The Problems of Philosophy*. The first stanza of 'The Effects' makes use of a line of Wallace Stevens's prose. 'A Blessing for the Big Men' borrows from Lady Gregory's translations of Raftery. The title headings in 'Progress' are taken from Bunyan's *Pilgrim's Progress*, as is its epigraph.

'Epithalamium': for Sarah Manguso and Adam Chapman.

'The Effects': for Paul Murdin.

'Progress': for Lorcan O'Neill.

Contents

Progress, 45

GO GIANTS

Epithalamium

You're beeswax and I'm birdshit.
I'm mostly harmless. You're irrational.
If I'm iniquity then you're theft.
One of us is supercalifragilistic.

If I'm the most insane disgusting filth
you're hardly curiosa.
You're bubblewrap to my fingertips.
You're winter sleep and I'm the bee dance.

And I am menthol and you are eggshell.
When you're atrocious I am Spellcheck.
You're the yen. I'm the Nepalese pound.
If I'm homesteading you're radical chic.

I'm carpet shock and you're the rail.
I'm Memory Foam Day on Price-Drop TV
and you're the Lord of Misrule who shrieks
when I surface in goggles through duckweed,

and I am Trafalgar, and you're Waterloo,
and frequently it seems to me that I am you,
and you are me. If I'm the rising incantation
you're the charm, or I am, or you are.

Condolence

Tucked up in the top bunk under my Spiderman duvet
I half-follow a story with a beginning and an end,

then she tiptoes the hallway to stand by the hearth
and considers, and sits, and slips the ruled sheet

behind the front page of her pad to write out in good
phrases to wives and the parents of husbands

with such slow deliberation the slack is blanched
and collapses, and the fire consumed by its ashes.

Santa Maddelena

Cool air massing on the mountain
passes through the ruled bamboo
with rumours of Etruscan archers
underneath our open window,
drawing arrows, creaking bows.

We are each other's provocation
and since noon no one has spoken.
Even to myself I seem like something
withstood, but it will be dark in ten,

and I'm glad the linden by the pool
yields in the breeze, then steadies,
ordering the tremor of its leaves
again to an unbroken canopy,
like the shields of legionaries.

Go Giants

Go go gadget legs. Go right. Go left.
Go wrong. Go west. Go down to the sea
in ships. Go down to the river and pray.
Go fish. Go first. Go forth and multiply.
Go in now and say goodbye. Go blind.
Go deaf. Go short. Go long. Go to press.

Go to pot. Go fuck yourself. Go straight.
Go Braves. Go jump in a lake. Go hard.
Go hide. Go down with a case of.
Go ape. Go without. Go Patriots.
Go halves. Go slow. Go under the knife.
Go under the sign of the war-shaft.

Go one better. Go great guns.
Go south. Go out in the midday sun.
Go red. Go blond. Go Vandals.
Go tell it on the mountain. Go and sin
no more. Go compare. Go nuclear.
Go back to E7 from E8. Go paperless.

Go Cowboys. Go Redskins. Go naked.
Go to ground. Go ahead. Go abroad.
Go to grass. Go slack. Go all ironic.
Go down in a blaze of. Go Titans.
Go for the sake of. Go Saints.
Go fly a kite. Go against. Go gaga.

Go in peace to love and serve the.
Go and get help. Go directly to jail.
Go down in flames. Go up in smoke.
Go for broke. Go tell Aunt Rhody.
Go tell the Spartans. Go to hell.
Go into detail. Go for the throat.

The Mark

In the Capitoline Museum

After that Etruscan she-wolf
tenting milk-fat twins, the grabby
cherubs added fairly awkwardly

around the time of Michelangelo,
we chance upon Marsyas, nearly dead.
Boxer's nose. Cow's lick. The arms tied

overhead are plain white marble,
as is the face, the beard, the gallows;
a petrified tree with prettified leaves.

The torso, though, is pavonazzetto;
the thin pink veins of which evince
a body, stripped of its skin.

*

Books tell you the Dorian mode
employed to worship Apollo
found its expression on lyres –

which the Phrygians refused,
preferring the music produced
by the reed-flutes cut from

the banks of the Marsyas River.
Though the death is not symbolic;
all pain's non-fictional,

based on the true story of pain.
Nature is precise in this.
It hurts as much as it's worth.

*

Also Apollo, the racist, cheated,
and the narrative's loaded by Greeks
who'd chosen the Dorian mode.

This is just the first triumph of the state
and the death of a human flautist,
whose large head is tilted forwards

and whose face bears such a dread expression
it served Renaissance painters as a template
for their crucifixion scenes – forgetting

of course that Christ sides with Apollo,
with all good sons of fractious gods
intent on implementing father's will.

*

There was the child who thought the darkness
in the branches was some stag that had got
its horns entangled, and thrashed itself in

deeper, to exhaustion and protracted death,
or someone from the town come
outside the walls to draw a tally line

beneath accounts for good this time,
but then he recognized him by
his substantial beard, the solid build,

and when the rug of flies shook out
he understood that all the skin
had been torn from him by some animal.

*

And since it predicts redress, is dilute with
the largesse of the much better informed,
the grief of Christ is inauthentic.

This is not. Marsyas only dropped in
to sit by the fire and play like a dream,
his calloused fingers pale darting

flames across the stops. But every tavern
has its own dog-killer and herd-god,
its bribe-swallower, its giver of luck –

and having got his pedigree,
having grasped the last injustice,
the mark was taken out the back and stiffed.

*

He dared a god and lost,
and got flayed alive for such presumption –
the river so-called arose from his blood

and the tears of his brothers and sons.
With no knife and only starlight
the youngest climbs, unties the knots

and sets the corpse free. The awful stench.
We wrap him in the swaddling cloths
and lug him uphill to an olive grove

that someone knows and in a little clearing
stack rocks around the body, then walk back
to a houseful of the vengeful and drunk.

Cabochon

She still has some cousins in Leitrim,
the tall nurse broadcasting our secret,
and bright eyes bright as trinkets
when her pink nail taps the screen.
Between the coda and the dipped head
a flicker in the quadrant's grain
steadies to a light bobbing
rhythmically, unhindered . . .

We stand before the elevator's
mirror now like any other passengers
disembarking at the gate, late,
a silent weight of uncut gems
stitched meticulously in the hems
of your winter coat, my leather case.

Envy

Nothing but admiration for that polar bear lying there flat out
as if he's punctured, and sea lions we also love who, like us,
suffer from that tic of always applauding their own tricks,

but I did detect again the same strained sadness in the eyes
of the apes and the larger monkeys, as if they felt they really
should become men, but could not discover the secret as to how

it happens – and who would not admit the background anguish,
sensing something better there almost within grasp but obvious,
the lack of wit and discipline and wherewithal preventing it

and in large despair I launch plots against my neighbour Gwen
who's also lost and carries round the same hot pennies of un-
happiness.   Gorilla, sir, I want to tell you we have surely

reached a stage in the evolving which is not the final stage,
and will pass through it quickly with dignity and grace,
acquiring something like the freedom of the universe.

Pershing

His high-ness. The foot-long hands. A suit that did not,
stiltwalker trousers and clown shoes, and localized in
the pliancy of the smile; embarrassment, kindness, the loss.
I tore out and Sellotaped the page to my wall, like an icon.

Now wire hair is growing from my ear canals and neck.
I tend to smell lightly of pine. The street's a hall of mirrors,
each reflection mine and brother wolfman, sister midget,
as I understand it we are metaphors of one another

and if I see the image of him loping down Tenth Avenue
or queuing in his anorak for coffee and a muffin –
his ducking, gentle, spectacled head an inch or two
from the wooden beam – I mean to look through him.

The Mission

You're on your own and walking down to Ryan's house and staring
hard at bags of rubbish thrown from cars on the old Dungannon road.
Overnight a revival tent has moored in the field as a rule reserved
for the circus or the vehicles of spectators for the *Cookstown 100*,
who picnic on the verge and cheer as motorbikes pass by in blurs,
in Doppler roars, and dip at the corner like fins or sails and right
again and disappear. You don't know what you're looking for.

You are sitting in the house alone in the unlit living room
with your Uncle Jack's double-barrelled split-piece shotgun
propped on velvet cushions and fed with scarlet cartridges
and pointing at the hallway, as a panel van revs in the drive
and someone tries forcing the back door. You keep a list
entitled *Bastards*, and when that spiral jotter's full you get
another and print with care *New Bastards* on the cover.

You are dragging loads of turf in white or brightly coloured
fertilizer bags from the outhouse to stack by the coal bunker,
and hear a human rumble coming from that tent tethered
three fields over. Gangs of midges gust and tremor above
the concrete slabs and a muddy lawn. You would like to be
any place else but watching Ryan crying like a little baby
as he stumbles down towards the stage to testify and get saved.

The Workshop

Her turgid sonnets.
His villanelle.
I will have my revenge,

and if I can't explain
precisely why I
do prefer to circumvent

the course our fathers,
those great nurslings,
drove their exhausted

steeds across, believe me,
something is coming.
Nightly I walk the strand

against the wind
and watch for it.

After Juvenal

Women in Antiquity

At the checkout Cleopatra.
Eyelash. Nailtap.
The Queen of Sheba leaving Tie Rack.

Boadicea clipping tickets.
Three Venuses of Willendorf
blocking the exhibit.

Is each of these figurines
meant to represent the goddess?
Or constitute an offering from votaries

by way of worship? You express
surprise at such a wide variety,
and I stay absolutely silent.

Each wood or stone statue stands
and holds her breasts or clasps
her hands above her solar plexus,

and though the guide itemizes reasons
against nakedness: social; shame;
the cold; aesthetic; to turn aside

the evil eye; the first four are
discarded easily enough in argument,
I think, but the eye is mine.

The Effects

from *The Catalogue of the Universe*

To see the gods withdraw,
dethroned, exposed to ridicule,
was our allotted truth –
and not without its suffering.

They weren't dislodged
by other, stronger gods:
they simply came to nothing.
That line of enquiry closed.

With space-time there are rules
on how to leave completely:
accrete, accrete, be massive,
wait, grow obsolete, begin

to shrink, speed up, cave in,
collapse and vanish –
and amid the photographs
of supergiants, red dwarfs,

the neon spiral nebulae,
is this rudimentary study done
with a compass and a pencil:
Black Hole (*Artist's impression*).

In modern death no light escapes.
You cannot see it only note
the wobble of the bodies
on their axes, in their orbits.

In Cookstown District Cemetery
hundreds pack the graveside till
mid-hymn, a dog gets free:
the animal I cannot see

only how the faces turn,
one-by-one and radiant,
to watch the mongrel running
masterless among them.

Tuesday

Me and a single mosquito
spend the evening in, suffering
a lightly withered baked potato
and the defunct aspect ratio:

all the ruins of Quintana Roo
slide in and out of lit bamboo
and *listen*, I tell the television,
who's standing in again for you,

Bring me the Rose of Jericho,
the left hook of Rocky Marciano,
a stampede of water buffalo
and an easier way to make sourdough
or fresh tortellini . . .

                   Don't. When I'm alone
I swear this whole thing's touch and go.

Annals of Alan

My carrel on the eighth floor of lower Manhattan has a lot
of graffiti devoted to Alan. **Alan has the best weed.**
Alan is a woman. The walrus is Alan. Do we still need Alan?
Alan I want to have your baby. Alan taped my nana.
Fuck Obama Alan for president.

Alan is Geraldo Rivera. The victory is Alan's.
I hate being Alan. Alan is a dream most likely.
Who the heck is Alan? Alan is homosexy.
Alan is a social construct. *I love Alan.*
It all comes down to Alan. I AM ALAN.

Alan is over. We are all Alan. Remember when
there was no Alan? If I am so beautiful and if you love me so
much then spell my fucking name correctly –
ALLEN. No, it's Allan. No, it's Alain.
Alain, Alain, t'es beau et je t'aime.

Donna

Her younger brother stole across the river
to boost beer kegs from the Royal Hotel
and float them back across the river –
and in accordance with all classical myth,
he hadn't bargained on the current.
The weirgate dredged him, dead.

Music was heaven to Donna, just heaven
overheard on earth, sifting down from
the shifting spheres or an open window,
the hi-hat moon. Heaven, with the heat
of evening, and her singing coming down
the stairs. Billie or Nina or Dinah.

Accompanying Death

The eyelids are generally half-closed;
the pupils dilated; the tongue approaches
the under-edges of the lips and these
are covered with a frothy mucus.

When the man in the eye turns away,
he becomes non-knowing of forms.
He does not see or smell or taste or speak
or hear. He does not think or feel.

Breathing and the heart's action cease.
Coldness and pallor of surface increase.

He slips into air that spins out and opens
to him as the hole in a chariot's wheel.

He does not see or speak or hear or feel.

He steals upwards, outwards, inwards.

Avi

They want to be happy, forgiven or healed.
Or a decent job in Tallahassee or Monroe.
Or enclose their numbers for the Big Sweep
next week even though they know He'll know.
One prays for his marriage to work. A sufferer
in stage four doesn't want her son to be alone.

I have come to *The Department of Dead Letters*,
correspondence that can neither be delivered
nor returned satisfactorily to the sender,
and this is the *Letters to God Division* –
which means a cardboard box and Avi Yaniv,
who runs it from a sorting office squashed between
a vacant car lot and a dry-cleaning business
on the outer outskirts of Givat Shaul,

and Avi, having slit open the colourless
envelope with his utility knife, unfolds once and unfolds
again to read how the writer asks from the sister she fought with
forgiveness – O Tatyana – who died the next day in a fall,

and our heavy-lidded bald employee Avi Yaniv,
sitting at his canteen table in a lemon-yellow polo shirt
and creamy cotton planting gloves,
refolds once and refolds again and sets the note
to one side, for delivery to the Western Wall.

He likes his work. He breaks for lunch. He talks about the post:
how an index card arrived last week with a shiny nickel
taped to it: 'I would like to thank you kindly for
this most amazing chance to participate in full
with regards to your one-off and exclusive offer
of prizes and awards in the Christian Faith.'

Some stay with him. The lonely, a Londoner,
who asked only for his recently deceased wife
to be returned to talk to in his dreams.
They tell him of terrible pain inside

O Rabi Jesus, His Reverence, The High Priest,
Great Lord, Dios, Muros de los Lamentos,
The Living Word, The Virgin Mary, Jesus Christ,
The Great Temple, The Holy One, Mein Gott,
Klagemauer, Israel, King David, Jerusalem,
Alpha, Omega, Almighty God

at night when I'm walking with the dog I find I'm
talking to the dog, and do you find that, I ask him.

Spree

The gardener mown down. The typist erased.
The postman dispatched and the vet put to sleep.
The fishmonger opened from anus to throat.
The binman wasted, bagged and disposed of.
The farmer led out like a lamb to the slaughter
and the son, the lost one, hanged from a beam,
is gathered at last to his mothers and fathers . . .

The butcher murdered. The baker butchered.
The candlestick-maker snuffed in his basement,
a flurry of blows to the back of the skull
with one blunt instrument, now missing,
since He's packed everything into his holdall
and calm, alert, efficient, left, not at all
discontented with how his day's looking.

Observance

Midway or Thermopylae
I watched the war couchant.
I watched the war on drugs
or drunk.

Geronimo. Banzai. Tallyho.
There is no catchword that I know
for the opposite of war,
a battle-cry

to herald only central heating
and four
triangles of buttered toast.
I watched the war supine

and saw the wars I watched
squared, and how,
and now
I watch the war concerned.

I mean the war in question.
Almost noon
when I declared and took
the field to walk the bitch

and carry back this lank posy
of cowslips,
and the hot soft ouroboros
of dogshit wrapped in plastic.

The Future

I can tell you that the organizing principle is grief.
You will lack weather. And if you sleep the dream
will just be a repeat of what you dreamt before,

the usual attempt to get somewhere fast on foot
as it grows clear – and also infinitely more obscure –
why you're exempt from ever getting there, why

every door you pass through only exits on another
flagstoned corridor, bordering another clean lawn
that seems the same one, and a jazz band's playing.

Still. Discernible beneath all that is the building-
site next door, and the high-pitched resistant tear
of one taut material moving through another.

Talking in Kitchens

Our friend Michael comes by and we sit at the table,
eating a curry from the Bombay Bicycle Club
and passing the baby between us.

When Michael has left we head upstairs
and the baby's asleep and we've talked ourselves out
and we feel as we feel every day of the year

like nobody knows how we feel and it's fine,
because our secrets live near the secrets of others,
and our wants are not so mean.

Easement comes in the weirdest of places
like that blue fire lit in the wood-burning stove
or the face on the dog when she chews at a carrot.

Here it is written down if I forget to say it –
my home is the temple made by your hands.

Special Effects

am sunk in velvet, surrounded by
the sound of violent doublethink;
sugar glass and blanks, such subterfuge
they use to skim meaning from the real,
but though the exit signs are dim

inside the auditorium,
exact attention will not fail
the ticks and bumps of icy cubes
blunting in your carbonated soft drink,
and mine, since at your side I

am sunk in velvet, surrounded by
the sound of violent doublethink;
sugar glass and blanks, such subterfuge
they use to skim meaning from the real,
but though the exit signs are dim

inside the auditorium,
exact attention will not fail
the ticks and bumps of icy cubes
blunting in your carbonated soft drink,
and mine, since at your side I

am sunk in velvet, surrounded by
the sound of violent doublethink;
sugar glass and blanks, such subterfuge
they use to skim meaning from the real,
but though the exit signs are dim

A Blessing for the Big Men

Health be to you since your camps were loosened;
it is men with God you are
and blessed is the earth you walked on.
The blessing of the sun and the moon be upon you.

I will go up on the mountain alone
and I will come hither from it again.
It is bonefires we used to have and playing-cards,
and the word of God was often with us –

It is not a little story this.
It is not the trouble of one house
or the grief of one harp-string.
A shelter to the naked. A comfort to the poor.

Och ochone!
O'Kelly has manuring for his land that is not sand or dung.

After Raftery

The Package from Latvia

I know no one in Latvia and have never been,
though I met up with a girlfriend in Vilnius once,
and years ago spent a druggy weekend in Tallinn
with my friend Tom, losing money in casinos
and buying two interRailers from Montreal
a flotilla of cocktails we couldn't afford.

But Latvia's a blank and this package, comparable
to a shoebox, maybe slightly bigger, has appeared
without a return address, and much postage of foreign fauna,
one stamp with a yellow bird on a blue background,
another that must be the flag.
                         I set it in the corner
beside the toaster and the broken kettle, and think about
a Canadian called Rain, who I expect no longer has a little
silver barbell piercing her left nipple.

Manifesto on Sunday

First of all, fuck the ignorant rat-faced girl giving backchat to the man in the vegetable shop for she's upsetting my sense of the world order. Second, fuck the man in the vegetable shop for he's more of a vegetable than the cauliflower. Third, fuck the banker unsure how to wire a plug for he's already reneging on what we agreed. Fourth, fuck the pundits for they talk too much and say nothing and will not explain in proper detail what they know and why or where and how they feel. Fifth, fuck the ballboys who expect me to buy this shit for they happily watched while the house got dismantled and we were left sat outside on a green Chesterfield and it looks like rain. Sixth, fuck the faith schools because I know what happens in the absence of others, and fuck all those who never got around to visiting the angry kings to state their queries plainly, but moped instead about the precinct, and fuck also the finest minds of my generation destroyed only by the soft lighting of advertising. Seventh, fuck those who want the licence fee cut. And eighth and ninth and tenth fuck this entire co-ordination since in any village A is working for B and C is really not feeling well at all and D, having misjudged the end of the steps, is mid-fall, his tray of coffee mug and coffee and digestive biscuits rising to their rest, then reaching it, then resting, then beginning to descend.

Adeline

When the smallest one among them
tasted air and named it breath,
the others lopped her silver hair
with garden shears and when she wept

all through the second hymn
they hid her yellow duffel coat
and so she ran the two streets home
to where they said they couldn't see her,

no. Her brother's glasses trapped the sun
and made his eyes alive with fire.
Each colour had a different flavour.
She ran the taps to free the rivers

then begged her eldest sister let her
count the galaxy of freckles.
But no one ever missed her
with their spit or snowballs,

an open hand or closed. She stayed
so still. She was so good.
They laid her body on the doorstep
like a sandbag for the flood.

Collusion

We'd wake to find the place
strange. Even some treeless
crossroads in the back end
of nowhere could, in a flash,
change: famous for a second
then synonymous with loss.

To commune, we knelt in packs
at altar rails on velvet pads
but still each pose was unalike:
head up; head down; dead tired;
frail; some arthritic twinge
or nerve trapped in the hip.

You might see from the aisle
the price stickers exposed
on the soles: mine, outsized,
were a man's black brogues
from Eastwoods' latest fire sale.
All ceremony is a hoax:

in bandit country the blackface
and cheviot, damp-fleeced, raddled,
wander unaware of entering
and exiting those great stone rings
archaeologists uncover, and claim
are like enough memorial.

Charm for Unfruitful Land

Eastward I stand and favours entreat.
I call the illustrious ones to yield;
the earth I beseech and each
of her keepers I summon to the field;

Mary, Christ, the blessèd Lord,
into your ears this glamour I pour.
From the teeth I speak each word.
Erce! Erce! Our Earth-Mother

let crops crop, let seeds seed,
and your yields yield to me. Let God
and every saint in heaven grant
my acres fortified against all slant

adversaries, their foul goetic means,
the demonry, the one-eyed spite,
all sortilege and jealousy
abroad like torches in the night:

I pray to Him who made this place,
no woman deft in conjuration
or man adept in talk and cunning
may halt the words I here unloose.

I praise the earth, the turf I hail,
the silt I stirred up I applaud;
the sod, the clod, the dirt, the soil,
the loam and clay I dig I laud,

I praise the use we put its fruits to,
commend provender, vittles, vivers,
whatever's lowered in on hooks to
cure and darken in the smokehouse,

whatever's threshed or dried or milled,
whatever's plucked or picked or caught,
whatever's raw or boiled or killed,
I drink, I eat, I smoke, I snort.

from the Anglo-Saxon

Grace and the Chilcot Inquiry

My daughter's two weeks old tonight
and my wife wants me to talk to her more
so I started to explain how the answer
I did the thing I thought was right
was enthymematic, and meant to obscure
another rather major conjecture viz.
I do the thing **I** *think it right to do.*

Her slow blinks mean that in democracies
the leader's not allowed to operate
according solely to what he or she decrees
is just or necessary; and my brand new
constituent looked appropriately cross
when I began to sing 'Amazing Grace'
to the tune 'The Sash My Father Wore'.

The Wonder

If the psalm house be possessed by saints, there would not come within the walls a man like enough to Magnus, bishop of here and all the north; a giant of holy innocence, the turtledove of charity, the wolfhound of courage and a casket of God's wisdom. A great wonder was wrought on the night he was taken – the land was a-blaze from the fall of Nocturn to the first call of the cock: a mass of fire-clouds arose and went west, and everyone a-woke and rose. Some say it never happened. Or that it was like that only by the sea, in the east, for a second. A week went past and the farmer MacGregor, son of the sister of Magnus, was found suffocated in a cave. We watched the bloody flux; mortalities. A feast. The great murrain of cows.

The Holy Cross of Rath-both rained blood from out its wounds, though distempers and diseases were not relieved thereby, and for five days we walked to see the whale cast up at Killybegs, and the three gold teeth found in its head. Lord Furnival died of an ulcer on his foot due to the miracles of Columcille and Brigid, and the other saints besides whose churches he had burnt. In the town of Sligo a goat gave birth to a piglet and the piglet gave birth to a stoat.

History of the Sonnet

Ten.
Nine.
Eight.
I was watching you from over there and I've got to say
    I think you're great.

Seven.
Six.
Five.
As the Latins say, seize the day and watch that dog
    and how time flies.

Four.
Three.
Two.
What I mean to say is I think I love you or anyway
    would love to fuck you.

One.
Sumthin' sumthin', sumthin' sumthin', sumthin'

Progress

Then said the Shepherds one to another, Let us here show the Pilgrims the Gates of the Celestial City, if they have skill to look through our Perspective Glass. The pilgrims lovingly accepted the motion: so they had them to the top of an high Hill, called Clear, and gave them their glass to look.

Then they tried to look; but the remembrance of that last thing that the Shepherds had shown them made their hands shake, by means of which impediment they could not look steadily through the glass; yet they thought they saw something like the Gate, and also some of the Glory of the place. Then they went away, and sang this Song.

(*City of Destruction*)

One thing I don't get used to is looking up
and seeing nothing, the heavens as gaunt
as a blanket thrown over a birdcage but

last night, back home, whole galaxies festooned
the sky outside my room, a few fields
and a stream and a deep lane from O'Neill's

old bawn, and a mile outside the market town
whose industries are matching; manufacturing
cement and processing the animals to meat.

(*The Dog*)

Down in the yard the Jack Russell barked
her co-ordinates out to an atmosphere
flecked like emery paper, the finest grade,

that whets the seriffed aerials and steeples,
sands carriageways and pastures flat. We
were warned not to deal with infinity

face to face: the icy bodies, the fire planets,
the swirling vast accreting gas giants,
all that spinning immaterial matter

like whether in Robert Alter's fine translation
Do not fling me from your presence
is verse eleven or verse twelve.

[47]

(*Hill Difficulty*)

Our mild and violent land of the giant
leylandii and four-bar bitumen fences.
Of porn mags stashed in blackthorn hedges.

The snout of a shotgun nuzzling out under
the valance as the eldest goes hoking for
presents from Santa beneath the bed.

Should Orestes just have been acquitted,
walked off scot-free? Not hard to get blood
from a stone if it's smashed in someone's face.

(*First Cause of the Hubbub*)

You can say courage but mean fear, and where
you place your secret kiss depend on chance,
on someone else's interpretations

of the books decreed in Rome in 382
to be the Gospel Truth.
The typical state is permanent war:

(*Mr Skill*)

All the cities of antiquity were walled
and minute observation saves us.
Galileo, plotting the trajectories

of four nomadic specks near Jupiter,
procured proof of a nature indisputable
That Not Everything Revolves Around You,

and this was the first disconnect between
the eye and fist, a new truth that soon
eclipsed the other facts that left you foxed

and slightly teary: funfair mirrors,
the central locking, a magnetic catch
on your mother's shiny leather purse.

(*Christian's Deplorable Condition*)

Say, 90% cement and 10% meat
when I moved to Rome at thirty
fairly hopeful, fairly certain I might

begin some sort of self-taught course in
Appreciating Beauty, on how not to view
it solely with incipient suspicion,

a Covenanter's eye to waste – in any case
I entered the belly of the beast:
city under occupation where each

(*Land of Vainglory*)

same-but-different priest would watch –
the pappy white hands clasped over the crotch –
as the checkout girl packed up his stuff:

Prosecco, zucchini, carta igienica –
and each time I wanted to obstruct,
like a friendly but finally menacing drunk,

and stand too close and interrupt and recount
at length how Tycho Brahe made himself
a metal nose, tipped with gold, and kept

beneath his table Jepp, the dwarf he thought
clairvoyant, and let his pet elk get so plastered
over dinner it stumbled down the stairs

and died.   I was thinking this:
that the history of history is ridiculous,
that these specifics were sufficient.

(*Plain Called Ease*)

You can reach down or up but you can't touch:
you live in the abstractions and this is
electricity. It flows on like a viscid

white river and this is how you contemplate
the density of stars, a breadcrumb on your sleeve
whose weight exceeds the Empire State –

and if what extends its living presence
from the Mariana Trench to out beyond
the last star's light, you have no name for,

or none for yet, even now you note
the continuity of things, how they mix
and bleed and how much trust there is implicit

in your fingertips, how history is hearsay,
shu-shu, bavardage, which you tend anyway
to read as a mirror or sexual trope:

(*Mr Brisk*)

A stranger arrives at night in the city
with something extraordinary under his cloak,
a leather pole that makes the most

distant bodies close. One could put one's eye
to the contraption, spy on washerwomen
spreading their apparel on the reeds to dry,

a button of horn on the torn shirt
of a steeplejack climbing the doge's palace.
He had to act fast and thought it out that night:

the shopping list, extant, reads: sheet glass,
an organ pipe, slippers for the boy, chickpeas,
artillery balls of variant size.

(*Hill Lucre*)

The Senate ascends the Campanile:
he'd worked the magnification up to ten
and could identify quite easily

which galleon it was threading the horizon
an hour or more from harbour – information
worth a purseful to the merchants

crowding the Rialto – and when he'd worked
up a few more mercantile triumphs,
Galileo trained his novel apparatus

on the night, and look, up close the moon
is not featureless and luminous
but scarred as a clean peach stone.

(*Giants Pope and Pagan*)

Urban the Eighth ordered all the birds
in the gardens of the Vatican be caught
in nets and killed, since their song disturbed

his concentration, and on the Ides of March
as he and the engineer from Pisa strolled
along the arboreal corridors, chaperoned

by apple blossom, bathed in speckled under-shade,
now freed into the sudden joy of green
noon-light, a taut attenuated

silence trailed behind them like a bridal train
of the whitest, finest silk . . . Friends still,
still respectful, still exerting considerable

pull on the other, as dense bodies will –
and an arrow's flight along the Tiber
Hugh O'Neill, the Great O'Neill

lay blind and crying out and dying
in a shuttered ground-floor stanza
of the Palazzo dei Penitenziari

(*Vanity Fair*)

(where four hundred years ahead
I would hear Eiléan Ní Chuilleanáin read,
still with no clue how her surname was said).

(*Valley of Humiliation*)

Because the problem with leaving home
is home follows, and by the time Tyrone
left, having exhausted his usefulness,

he had been baited to his beard and mocked,
the lands lost, his rights to hunt and fish lost . . .
Fake obeisance, real fear, such dissimulation:

all that saps the character, infects the will
and the greatest danger to the English
since the time of Silken Thomas dwindled

in the warm south; his sight began to go;
he slept with an unsheathed sword by his side
and drank too much, and remembered, and attended

to matters with great pride and a little shame,
drafting letters home, complaining and battling with
Lombard, plotting the Spanish Ambassador's visit:

and those of us left eventually annexed
the fort at Tullyhogue for hide-and-seek,
then menthol cigarettes and adolescent sex.

(*Mount Clear*)

A roll-bar cattle grid in the car park
and steeply up to a flat-topped hillock,
a ring of trees sunlight besieges.

Outwards lies Tyrone: its working dogs,
its dreary steeples, its thousand and one
standing stones graffitied, out of plumb,

and in here the remains of a small fire
and you go further and further round
until your hands can pioneer her

wrists, her neck, her bra, her waist, her lips
a little gluey with the apricot
lip balm from the Body Shop in Castle Court.

(*Enchanted Ground*)

The noise of the breeze in the leaves is enormous.
The sound is the sound of an ocean
you stand at the edge of, an Atlantic unseen

with the naked eye but which you can taste
in the saltiness faint on her neck, on her breasts:
and amid the clang of bucklers, a hundred

harps aflutter, the Great O'Neill was crowned
atop the hill of Ireland's Youth . . . You grin
and lie flat out, shaded, lit, assuaged, watching

sky and supple leaf-print, holding and defending
nothing but the unzipped and unstrapped pitch-
perfect one beside you humming something

by the Smiths and tracing lightly cursive
shapes with a finger on your inside wrist.
A dandelion seed slides along its rill of air

and rises and rises and passes from sight.
Home is only one depiction of reality
and there are others, yes, but this is mine.

I look out from two nail-holes six feet up.
Most of my skin is lacking nerve endings
and my hearing's much worse than the dog's but –

(*Mr Implacable*)

as to how I might attest to *presence* –
that thing lit and extraordinary –
I would cite the not infrequent

visits of the dandelion seed, aloft, adrift,
proceeding, streeling above Paradise,
ten thousand houses of the saddest news

where the lion's tooth, unloosed, brings
the same sensations of translucency
I experienced a lot on Zoloft and vodka

or Zispin and whiskey
and in certain passages of Ammons
or Edmund Burke or Wallace Stevens.

(*Country of Conceit*)

Here or there in the Benthic dip or cloud
conjecture I don't think I'm exactly lost
but I couldn't, at this juncture, point due north,

or tell you if the ground below the paving
underneath my dealer boots is clay or sand
or rock, or what phase the moon is in.

(In phonetics a 'juncture' is the set
of features that let a listener detect
a word or phrase boundary, which means

distinguishing between, say, *I scream*
and *Ice cream*. It is a tiny interstice
but I am persistent, and it fits

(*Porter Watchful*)

since I kept beneath my bed a bayonet
from Passchendaele and a Reader's Digest
telescope wrapped up in a scout blanket

bedizened with embroidered badges
designating all the other youngsters
stationed at their outposts, ready.

The spyglass, enamelled navy, plastic-
capped with black, offered up the prolonged drop
into the cosmic well wherein there shone not

a single pebble of quartz in the depths
but hundreds and thousands and millions
all glittering and still insisting.)

(*House of the Interpreter*)

Marilyn-obsessive and ex-brickie
my cheerfully miscast Reverend Twomey
gave me the lend of the *Flashman* series,

his *Ed McBain*s and *Modesty Blaise*s
and I would devour them under cover
with a dying torch or in the summer

with the curtains left ajar, just a touch –
before I'd slide back out to readjust
and readjust their patterning of Spiderman

so it didn't seem too like a spider,
or a man, that dutiful dead-eyed intruder
whose desperate extended hands . . .

The Wonderful Story of Henry Sugar
and Bronowski's *The Ascent of Man*
salvaged from the Save the Children.

(*Mr Self-Will*)

My Dad gave me a biography of one
Willie John MacBride, not the drunk vain
murderous lout but Ireland's lock from Toome,

captain of the Lions on their finest tour
against the Boer, that, and a leather-
bound set of Somerset Maugham

he'd bought by accident at auction,
thinking he was bidding on
a lovely solid oak sideboard.

(*Chastised by a Shining One*)

David, I am getting to it.
If you would give me just a minute.
An ability to pull the graceful pint and tend

a bar I owe to you, my useful skill,
and the one which saw me mostly liquid
through my college years and law school.

You had come back for a spell from Australia
to see Annie, your mother, who'd suffered a scare,
and even there, by that, showed me the ropes.

(*Fierceness of the Lions*)

(BTW MacBride's test series was won
three-nil with one game drawn. Management,
noting how the Saffas liked to browbeat

their opponents with physical aggression,
and aware a player's substitution
was only possible if a doctor

certified him unfit to stay on the pitch,
and since there were no sideline officials
or cameras to keep punches and kicks

and headbutting to a minimum,
determined on the strategy that if
a Springbok should start to come

the big man and chance his hand, the Lions
were to call ninety-nine as a signal
for the entire team to fly in

hard with elbows and studs and fists,
acting as a single animal,
and get all of their retaliation in first.)

(*Mr Malice*)

If you're interested, a neat routine
for experiencing a fair selection
of the atoms of the known universe

is just to breathe in, and wait a bit,
and then breathe out, and as I do this,
I'm listening to *Miserere mei, Deus*

on repeat, and sitting back in bed
in Rome, in my fourth-floor walk-up
five minutes' stroll from that unlighted

and very cool interior with a Caravaggio,
above the basement room they brought Galileo to
and showed the instruments they'd use:

thumbscrews, the rack, the brodequin,
the judas cradle, the prayer stool . . .
The recording's sung in the cathedral

of the city I arrived in one thundery wet
Sunday night already late and homesick,
if adamant on working out how best

I might defect, how else I might backslide
on god and spurn the tribe and go outside
and slam the door behind me, hard.

I would set forth as music might
the history of the province, I mean
with passion and without meaning.

(*Reliever*)

I mean once more with feeling. I mean
Allegri composed it at the commission
of Pope Urban, who reserved it for use

in the Tenebrae service during Holy Week,
that 3 a.m. sequence when the candles
are extinguished in the Sistine Chapel

one by one, until a single drop of flame
remains – and it is a fine baroque example
of how successfully the choral template

might adjust itself to fit an elliptic
non-contiguous life, since it embodies
what it indicates, and so the unison is

queried repeatedly with descant:
four songsters counter five – one slow chant
builds and then, across the chancel, a slant account

occurs – and when those other voices enter
it is like water meeting water
which forces some new channel open in

the mind – silvers, slivers, shafts and ribbons,
countershafts and anabranch, rills and winterbourne –
and each discrete human voice uncaps

a separate grade of light so when the counter-
tenor rests for four beats on the top C
you fall slightly upwards and desire to be clean.

(*Valley of the Shadow*)

David, it's been twenty years
and I hardly remember your face.
Your tremendous hair I do remember,

a kind of feather-cut highlighted mullet,
and your taste for the shoe-string leather-thong
neckties favoured by Mexican cattlemen.

The clip-clop of your cowboy boots.
The fury all goes somewhere and I'm sorry
about this. You were always a bit

self-conscious – as I was, and as I am
starting in the bar, fourteen and withdrawn
and gangly, and you're patient enough

with changing the barrels and cleaning the lines.
You banged on about the outback's open
endless roads, the shimmering heat and the red light

and the absolutely empty desert,
but you were only travelling back from Omagh
with the others, dayshifting with a roofer.

Our windows pulsed once, twice, but didn't break.
You had the right firmness, could make a joke
and still say no, and had grown stout enough

to be thumped or hugged or roughhoused
by any drunk at the weddings we'd do –
that we did – but you couldn't handle this.

When I drove past the brass plaque the last time
I saw some
had defaced it with a marker pen again.

(*Giant Despair*)

After that sustained top C you're jittery
as a compass needle, until the plainsong
starts again and the choruses are calling

forth responses from the other side:
the singing has the force of argument,
though since the final verse is sung by

(*Man in an Iron Cage*)

both choirs in harmony, an argument
concluding in something shared and singular,
like sleep or being human, subject

to that death – and why coax us in like that God?
Why the bait, the switch, the ambuscade?
(From the Latin, *to place in a wood*).

Writing it down or performing it elsewhere
meant excommunication: this is dream
logic. In mine, a family gathering.

I mean the family plot. I mean two down
from Allingham at St Anne's in Ballyshannon.
Mise Eire. Meh! Deuce.

(*Mr Enmity*)

In Cookstown once upon a time
a Church of Ireland schoolboy trudging home
did cross the road and pass the chapel gates

and cross himself and pass into the cracked
looking-glass where he felt safe and oddly dangerous.
For many years my nemesis was Fergus

who waited like a suitor in the afternoon
after school with his lot by the bus stop.
I was tall for the fourth form and thin

and wore the wrong uniform for him.
As did he for me. Like MacBride.
Both of them! This is becoming a theme!

The monotony of always being on a side!
By the picture-house he blacked my eye
and in The Golden Bowl I split his lip.

And if I took some pleasure in it then
I don't remember. I'd note I had been met
and left with an excess of aggression.

I had been held against a wall and spat on,
torn my skin and clothing on barbed
wire as I fled. I had been scared.

(*Giant Grim*)

And it was real disaster (*astra*, stars)
that Fergus stood on the cutting floor
of the meatplant where I spent my summers

moping on the packing line, lugging plastic
crates of feathercut and paddywhack
and prime off the belt and onto the palettes,

and then wrapping each stacked tower with
the massive roll of clingfilm Americans
call cellophane. Brian wasn't listening;

having spent the morning absorbed
in constructing a skull-sized silver orb
by sticking gaffer tape around itself,

he was playing keepy-up and keeping
count when I got the word to head down
to see the foreman Mighty Quinn . . .

(Mr Hold-the-World)

I would like to see Mozart in the Sistine,
watching the darkness arrange itself
as the candles are damped one by one,

chewing a hangnail, half-thrilled and half-bored
to be taking the music apart in his head.
His quill scratching it out on the starched

parchment later and his fingers stained black
with the cuttlefish ink, not with ash,
but black anyway as the hand of Prometheus.

(By-Path Meadow)

If it is a number, it's irrational.
Like the square root of two. Or pi.
It doesn't die. It's memory, a memory

feat. It is discrete and doesn't stop.
It doesn't stop, that is, until it does:
it dies. A man, the son of Someone,

is killed in his own town by anagrams
of nativist and visitant. Amen.
And the Baron of D etc.

Any number, even Constant, has its patterns.
Keep an eye skinned for something to sharpen
as you mooch along the tarmac, something

[65]

to lob or to burn, for some fact to report
apart from the porn left in the hedge,
the own-brand bottles of vodka smashed against

the stop sign or the same unfamiliar
green Sierra parked up by the piggeries
for the fourth or fifth evening in a row.

You stand on the verge for the tractor to pass
and trail a long stick to poke roadkill with
or the dozen fertilizer bags of stiff

gawpy chickens your sister saw young Morgan –
the one not right in the head, not the one
in prison – chucking off the Red Bridge.

(*Valley of Humiliation*)

In his medieval chainmail apron
Fergus was again waiting, with Beetle
O'Donnell and Mungo, and an arsenal

of animals dismantled, unhitched
from tendon and skin, the glistening
testicles, kidneys, livers, the slick

rippling hearts – I heard the door bolt
behind, and began to run before
I'd even reached the cutting floor.

All trajectories are parabolic,
and Galileo demonstrated how
metal spheres fired from a falconet

will come to earth in line with gradient
and force. As far as it goes, the problem
isn't stumbling on the proper emblems

but being quick enough to dodge them –
and the boiler suits were dyed bright red
so you'd hardly notice the splatters of blood.

(*Wicket Gate*)

That lunchtime Fergus ate my sandwiches
and left my Mid-Ulster Mail torn up in
little printed petals on the wood-grain

of the melamine table. The canteen
fell silent when I came in and sat down
and looked up and did nothing.

(*Gaius's Inn*)

David, it's 3 a.m. and I am done.
I've turned all the bottles outwards
in the fridge below the till and you are

crossing the deserted parquet dance floor,
boot heels tapping, carrying a dustpan,
in the other hand a stacking chair –

(*The Arbour*)

I should say there is this density to objects,
and that they gather weight in time and spin
on without effort in their orbits gaining

[67]

traction, gravity and drag, a fullness in the
sense of things, and always drawing other
objects closer with a pull that lifts the whole

of you and sees you in safe and sound at home to
die a good death with family round you.
Fallacious, that, and what powers live on through us,

ordering their preferments and our lies,
do not give two fucks for us. We do as we are told.
The stars are hard and deaf and cold;

the river unconcerned about our presence
or its absence, and to paraphrase the meaning
is depletion of that meaning: even a one-to-one

map would lack both depth and texture: nicknames,
the favourite chocolate in the box of Roses,
how someone dries herself or dresses

after the shower, slowly, piece by piece,
wandering the flat on the phone to her sister,
all life's boring secret lovely histories,

minutiae of the dying who simply go on
dying now forever, the fixed blur of a spun
thing which spins so fast the focus of the eye

(*Mr Honest*)

cannot alight on it, can't print an image
on the retina but is repeatedly flung
off and forced by motion into motion.

Imagine how he sets the spared artillery ball
at the centre of the wheel to grind the lens,
how he pedals and then delicately leans

sheet glass into the metal surface so it shrieks
and sparks glitter out and he waits and then leans
the changed sheet of glass away . . .

(*House Beautiful*)

What if you felt nothing more walking down
the streets of Cookstown than you ever felt
walking in New York or Rome or London,

that you knew no one and the plenitude
of faces meant an openness and soft regard
for all the local gods, some dulling into love

by constant movement, children, music, dogs,
by the caramel or black or light pink
skin the people move and keep on moving

the miraculous flesh of their bodies in.

Nick Laird was born in County Tyrone in 1975 and educated at Cambridge University. For many years he worked as a lawyer before leaving to write poetry and fiction full-time. He writes and reviews for many newspapers and journals and teaches at Princeton University. He has published three poetry collections: *To a Fault* (2005), *On Purpose* (2007), and *Go Giants* (2013), and two novels: *Utterly Monkey* (2005) and *Glover's Mistake* (2009). His awards include the Rooney Prize for Irish Literature, the Geoffrey Faber Memorial Prize, the Betty Trask Prize, and a Somerset Maugham Award. He is a Fellow of the Royal Society of Literature.

More Praise for *Go Giants*

"An intricately woven display of memory, passion and learning . . . impressive . . . startling." —*Sunday Telegraph*

"Both playful and powerful . . . wonderful. . . . At his frequent best he finds the right voice to address and calm the fears of past and future times." —*Daily Telegraph*

"Undoubtedly [Laird's] most accomplished, fully realised and ambitious collection to date . . . fiercely intelligent and persuasive. . . . It's only fitting that it is a poet of Laird's skill who reminds us of the rewards that are reaped by language that is hard won and powerfully executed." —*Irish Post*

"*Go Giants* is both passionate and thoughtfully constructed. Anyone with an interest in the continuing evolution of Irish poetry will want to read it." —*Irish Times*

More Praise for *On Purpose* and *To a Fault*

"Loquacious, voluble, able to revel in details. . . . Laird's ear for 'smallish lexical mercies' yields superb lines."
—Stephen Burt,
New York Times Book Review

"Dammit, this is what a poetry collection should be: pained but sturdy, raw but dignified, lyrical but never fussy. *On Purpose* . . . will knock you flat." —Dave Eggers